Dinkum Aussie Slang

John Meredith

Dinkum Aussie Slang

A Handbook of Australian Rhyming Slang

Kangaroo Press

Acknowledgment
The author thanks Chris Woodland and others who
supplied additional items for the second edition.

drawings by George Sprod

Reprinted 1993
First published in 1984 as Learn to Talk Old Jack Lang
This edition first published in 1991 by Kangaroo Press Pty Ltd
3 Whitehall Road (P.O. Box 75) Kenthurst 2156
Typeset by G.T. Setters Pty Limited, Kenthurst 2156
Printed in Singapore by Kyodo Printing Co (S'pore) Pte Ltd

ISBN 0 86417 333 4

Contents

Curry and rice

Australian Rhyming Slang

History and Background

Contrary to general supposition, rhyming slang did not come down to us from our convict forbears and has no connection with the thieves' argot, flash talk, or vulgar tongue of the 18th and 19th century.

Price Warung, in his stories of the convict days in general, and in particular, that thrilling *Secret Society of the Ring* yarn, describes the secret language used by the prisoners. He provides some examples of their talk, but in them there is not so much as a hint of rhyming slang.

James Hardy Vaux, surely one of the most remarkable convicts ever to be transported to this country, compiled his *Vocabulary of the Flash Language* at Newcastle in 1811. It was included in his *Memoirs*, published in 1819 and consists for the most part of London thieves' cant, but, again, no rhyming slang whatever.

Another such dictionary, Captain Grose's *Dictionary of the Vulgar Tongue*, first published in London in 1811 is similar in nature to Vaux's *Vocabulary*, both in its content and in that it also does not mention rhyming slang nor does it provide any examples.

A poem by the humorist, W.T. Goodge, written in 1897 has 56 lines made up completely of slang terms current at that time. Titled *The Great Australian Slanguage* it provides numerous gems of slang from the shearing sheds and the city pushes, yet again, not one example of what is known in the argot as "Old Jack Lang".

Its first arrival in this country is described by Sidney J. Baker in his book *The Australian Language*:

> However, in 1898, a writer points out: 'The Cockney rhyming slang is popular in Australia and the lion comiques and lydies[sic] of the variety stage are helping to make the hold stronger.' The following examples were added to show the type of rhymes used—*Arty Rolla*, a collar; *mince pies*, eyes; *cheese and kisses*, the missus; *Charlie Prescott*, waistcoat; *Joe Morgan*, street organ; *pot and pan*, the old man; *tiddley-wink*, a drink; *lamb's fry*, tie; *lump o'lead*, bread; *plates o'meat*, the feet.

In the *Australian Magazine* of November 1, 1908, J.H. Garth noted that rhyming slang "broke out a couple of years ago".

Thus, it would seem that this sort of slang became popular at the turn of the century.

Baker has an interesting theory, that rhyming slang has had brief vogues in Australia, and that its periods of popularity have coincided with the wars. Thus, it was initially introduced at the time of the Boer War and has had resurgent waves of increased usage during the 1914–18 war and again at the time of the 1939–45 conflict.

Is this because, with minor exceptions, its use generally is a male prerogative? And that its increased use occurs when men are thrown together more than is usually the case, and is evidence of a form of camaraderie or tribal behaviour?

This certainly would appear to be the case with the use of rhyming slang in times of peace. During these periods it is most popular in places where men are gathered to the exclusion of the fair sex, such as shearing shed, jail, the race course and the pub. It is also much used in men's isolated work-camps.

The author has met only one woman who was fluent in the use of this form of slang, and she was one who had "done time". Does this mean that some ladies also, when isolated from the opposite sex become proficient in its use?

It is a point of interest that the example provided by Duke Tritton's *Flash Talk Letter* is dated 1905, about the period when J.H. Garth states that rhyming slang "broke out".

The collection of Australian rhyming slang presented in this book has been noted down from oral sources in and around Sydney during the past 20 years. Three of my best informants were mates who had spent some years as guests of Her Majesty in Sydney's Long Bay Jail. Two other prolific sources were a couple of retired shearers, the late Jim Loftus of Surry Hills and the late Duke Tritton of Concord.

WHAT IS IT?

Basically, rhyming slang consists of a couplet or short phrase of two, three, or more syllables, the last of which rhymes with the word for which the phrase is substituted. Often there is a droll association of the original word and the substitution, *e.g. Cries and screeches* for leeches; *gay and hearty* for a party, and *Jack Scratches* for matches.

An interesting feature is the use of disguise, or a contraction of the slang phase, so that instead of saying *elephant's trunk* for drunk, one simply says *elephants*; or to indicate an intention of urinating, "I'm going for a *snakes*", by which it is understood that you are going for a *snake's hiss*, or a piss.

Rhyming slang is always explicit. Thus there are words which in certain old fashioned or "refined" circles might be regarded as coarse, or even obscene. Other terms may even be interpreted as having racist connotations.

It should be remembered that these words, in some cases stood for other slang words which were in general popular use earlier in the century in an inoffensive and non-aggressive way. "Wog", "Dago" and "Chow" certainly are not in general acceptance today, yet in the author's childhood they were always used. "Charlie the Chow" was our vegetable man, and we always went down to the "Dago's" to buy our penny ice cream cone.

Other terms might even be objected to on sexist or even religious grounds. They are included in this collection simply because it is a record of what rhyming slang has been spoken in Australia since its introduction, and what is still used in certain circles today. To delete these terms on moral grounds would be an unacceptable act of censorship that would result in a distorted historical record.

I have therefore, included all the rhyming slang terms which I have collected, including a few obsolete names from the old monetary system, even although the latter may present a puzzle to some of the younger generation.

This book contains two vocabularies. The first gives the slang terms with their "straight" meanings. A second list translates "straight" words into rhyming slang terms. The Duke Tritton letter to his mate was discovered among his papers when the author was researching material for the biography of that grand old man recently published under the title of *Duke of the Outback*.

Since rhyming slang obviously had its beginnings in the music halls of East London, many of the terms will be survivors from that source in the early part of the century. Possibly a few originated with Americans who were stationed here in the early 1940s, but the majority constitute a fascinating part of the Australian vernacular.

There are of course varying levels of skill in its use. Recently the author was conversing with one skilled "linguist" who used "aris" for "arse". Asked to justify its usage, he replied: "Well, Aristotle is a bottle; bottle-and-glass is an arse, Aris is short for Aristotle, so therefore an Aris is an Arse!"

A snake's hiss

Duke Tritton's Rhyming Slang Letter

Woop Woop,
Beyond the Black Stump.
Mar. 3rd 1905

Dear *China Plate*,

No doubt you have wondered how your old *thief and robber* has been doing since you went back to the *steak and kidney*. I know you will find it hard to believe, but I am now a married man.

I think I had better tell you the *grim and gory* right from the *horse and cart*. When I saw you off on the *thunder and rain* at Weenia, I was feeling pretty lonely being left on my *Pat Malone*. So I rambled over to the *rubbity dub* and had a pint of *oh my dear*. In fact I had several and finished up in the dead house, broke to the wide. But they left me my *Willy Wag* and gave me a bit of tucker.

So I padded the hoof along the *frog and toad*, still feeling *butcher's hook*. I saw a lot of *Joe Blakes*, but don't know if they were dinkum or just the after effects of the grog. I came to a *bullock's liver* where I reckoned I'd have a *lemon squash* and liven up a bit. So I threw off my *barrel of fat*, *dicky dirt*, *rammy rousers* and *daisy roots*, and dived into the *mother and daughter*. It was *brave and bold*, and there were plenty of *cries and screeches*, but when I rubbed the *Cape of Good Hope* over myself, they went. I felt goodoh when

I came out and dried myself with the *Baden Powell*. So I gathered some *do me good*, got out the *Jack Scratches* and lit the *Barney Maguire*, put on the *knock me silly* and made a brew of *Jimmy Lee*.

Then I began to live again. The *hot cross bun* was down and the *silver spoon* was rising when I spread the Wagga and turned in. Next morning I was ready to move when a *pot and pan* driving a nice high stepping *tomato sauce* in a flash *big an' bulky* pulled up and asked if I was looking for *dodge an' shirk*. Being as flat as a goanna drinking at a Billabong I replied, "My blanky oath". "Well," he said, "I want a man that knows farm work and can shear blades or machine." I answered, "Mate, I know farm work backwards, and as for shearing I can blind Tom Power with wool with the Wolseleys and give Jacky Howe fifty start with the blades any day in the week. (You remember *China*, I was never backward in coming forward.)

He laughed and said "Well I really don't want a man that good, but if twenty-five bob and tucker is any good to you, hop in." I hopped in. We drove about ten miles to his place and he introduced me to his *cheese and kisses* and four *tin lids*, two *mother's joys* and two *twist and twirls*. When I remarked he had a nice little family, he said "My eldest is inside. Come in and meet her." We went in and I met her. She put out her hand and said "How do you do". My *grocer's cart* was racing like grandfather's clock when it slipped out of gear. After about ten seconds I managed to croak something that sounded like "Pleased to meetcha".

Straight wire, *China*, she is the most beautiful *ocean liner* I ever saw. Her name is Mary. Her *Dublin fair* is sort of brown, her *mince pies* are blue, her *north and south* was made for kissing and from the top of her *lump of lead* to her *plates of meat* she is perfect. And six months ago she became my *trouble an' strife*. Sometimes I wonder why she married me, and when I ask her, she just smiles and says "It must have been because of your good looks". (Which is kidding as you know I am no oil painting.)

I have tossed my *cherry ripe* into the *Barney Maguire* and I have given the *mud and ooze* right away. I can go into the *rubbity dub* and have a lemonade, breasting the *near and far* with booze hounds drinking *Tom Thumb*, *young and frisky*, *oh my dear*, or *Huckleberry Finn*, and no one ever laughs at me or calls me sissy because I am drinking lolly water. I hope they don't ever forget themselves, because Mary doesn't like the idea of me fighting. She thinks it is brutal.

I go to *roll and lurch* every Sunday, and the *Winchcombe Carson* reckons I've got a bosker *lets rejoice*, and often gets me to sing *hers an' hims* on my *Pat Malone*. And I like meeting the *spire and steeple*. They are all nice blokes and sheilas.

And I can come home now after a hard day's yakka, change into clean duds, shove my *Dutch pegs* under the *Cain and Abel*, wade through half a dozen dishes of scran that we used to dream of when we were on the track, then finish up with *Uncle Ned* and *roll me in the gutter*. No doubt about it, my Mary is a bottling *babbling brook*.

And I am popular with the family, and the neighbours. So everything is jakalorum. I'm teaching Mary and all the *tin lids* in the district to *dark an' dim*, and they reckon I'm the bees knees, ants pants and nits tits all rolled into one. If I speak of Barney Keiran, Alick Wickham or the Cavells, they reckon I could give any one of them ten yards in a hundred.

My father-in-law (Gor blimey, just fancy me having a father-in-law) built a nice cottage for Mary and me, so we are as snug as bugs in a rug, and it seems that the only troubles we are likely to have are little ones.

It is hard to believe that two years ago I was humpin' the drum with you, spending all my *Oscar Asche* on *mud and ooze*, and two-up, fighting and brawling, stoushing *John Hops*, getting run in and spending a few days in the cooler, pinching the squatter's lambs when we were out of meat, jumping the rattler and acting all round like a pair of half witted clowns.

I told Mary it would be nice to have you up here for a holiday, but she is not real keen on the idea because she thinks you have been a bad influence in my life, and you might lead me astray again. Which just goes to show how innocent she is.

Well *China*, this *don't forget her* is getting long and I am out of *nails and screws*, and I have to catch the *Holy Ghost*, so will end off with all the best from,

Your old *thief and robber*,
Duke

Vocabulary

Rhyming Slang to "Straight"

Bag of fruit

A

A.I.F.: deaf

Adrian Quist: pissed, drunk

African nigger: cigger., cigarette

Al Capone: 'phone, the telephone

all stations: an Alsatian (dog)

Alma Grey: a trey, threepence (obs.)

almond rocks: a pair of socks

Alsatian dog: Wog, an Italian

Amos and Andy: brandy

Andy Capp: a crap, to defecate

Andy Maguire: a fire

angel's kiss: a piss

Annie Louise: cheese

apple sauce: a horse

apple tart: a fart (he apple tarted)

apples and pears: stairs

April fool: the tool, penis

Aristotle, Aris: a bottle

arse over header: the varsovienna, a dance

arsehole of the goanna: the varsovienna, a dance

Auntie Meg: a keg, keg of beer

B

babbling brook, babbler: a cook

Baden Powell: a towel

bag of fruit: a suit

ball of twine: railway line

barmaid's blush: a flush, as in poker

Barney Maguire: a fire

barrel of fat: a hat

bat and ball: a wall

Beecham's Pill: a dill, a fool

bees and honey: money

Betty Grable: a table

bib and bub: a tub, e.g. **have a bib and bub:**   take a bath

big and bulky: a sulky

bird's lime: the time

blood blister: sister

Bo Peep: sleep

Bob Hope: soap

Bob Powell: a towel. See also **Baden Powell**

Bobby Martin: a carton

bobby rocks: a pair of socks

bona fide: terrified

boots and sock: the pox

Botany Bay: to run away, e.g. **do a Botany**

bottle and glass: the arse

bottle and stopper: a copper, policeman

Brahms and Liszt: pissed (drunk)

brave and bold: cold

bread and jam: a tram

Bristol cities, Bristols: titties

Brown Joe: in the know

bubble and squeak: a leak, to urinate

Bugs Bunny: money

bullock's kidney: Sydney

bullock's liver: a river

bundle of socks: think-box, the head

butcher's hook (1): feeling crook

butcher's hook, butchers (2): a look,
  e.g. **take a butchers at this**
buttons and bows: toes

C

cabbage tree hat: a rat, an informer
Cain and Abel: a table
Cape of Good Hope: soap
Captains Bloods: spuds, potatoes
Captain Cook: a look
cash and carry: to marry
cast a net: have a bet
cats and mice: dice
cattle dog: a catalogue
cattle ticks: Catholics
Charlie Britt: a fit. e.g. **throw a
  Charlie**
Charlie Chase: a race. e.g. **not in the
  Charlie** = not worthy of consideration
Charlie Wheeler, Charlie: a sheila
cheese and kisses: the missus, e.g. **the
  old cheese**
cheesy kiss: a miss; a missed catch at
  cricket
cherry ripe: a smoking pipe
china plate, china: a mate
chock and log: a dog
Chocolate frog: a Wog, an Italian
Christmas card: train guard
chuck me in the gutter: butter
chunk of beef, chunka: the chief, the
  boss

clickety-click: a stick

clothes pegs: the legs

coalbox: the chorus (of a song)

Cobar shower: a flower

cobbler's awls, cobblers: balls, testicles, or Balls! = Rubbish!, Nonsense!

Coca Cola: a bowler, in cricket

cockies' clip: a dip = a pick-pocket, or a swim

Coffs Harbour: a barber

comic cuts: the guts

constant screamer: a concertina

cotton wool: a pull, to masturbate

cough and sneeze: cheese

cow's hoof: a poof, poofter, male homosexual

cricket bats: the tats, teeth

cries and screeches: leeches

cry and laugh: a scarf

cucumber: a number

cuff link: a drink

curly locks: socks

currant bun: the sun

curry and rice: the price

D

Dad and Dave: a shave

Dad and Mum: rum, Bonox and rum

daisy roots: boots

Darby and Joan: a loan

Darby Kelly: the belly

dark and dim: a swim

darling it hurts: Darlinghurst

dark felt: a belt

Dawn Frazer: a razor

dead horse: sauce

dead wowsers: trousers

deaf and dumb: the drum, inside information, e.g. **'I'll give you the deaf and dumb'**

Derby winner: a dinner

dibs and dabs: crabs (body lice)

Dicky Lee (1): a pee, to urinate

Dicky Lee (2): tea

dig a grave: have a shave

dingaling: the king

dinky dirt: a shirt

Dinny Hayes-er: a king hit = a shit

dip and chuck it: a bucket

dip and duck it: a bucket

dirt grime and dust: crust (on a pie)

dirty dish: fish

do me good: firewood

docker's hook: a book, i.e. **make a docker's hook:** to lay the odds or make a book.

dodge and shirk: work

dog and bone: the phone

Donald Duck: a fuck

don't be funny: a dunny, lavatory

don't forget her: a letter, a French letter

Doris Day: a gay, homosexual

Dorothy Dix: a six, in cricket

Dorothy Gish, Dorothy: a dish

down and up: a cup
dribs and drabs: the crabs, body lice
Dublin Fair: the hair
ducks and drakes: the shakes, D.T.s
ducks and geese: the police
duck's neck: a cheque
Dutch peg(s): leg(s)

E

Eau de Cologne: the 'phone
Edgar Britt: a shit
egg and spoon: a goon, a silly person
egg flip: a tip, in horse racing
Eiffel Tower: a shower
eight-day clock: the cock, penis
elephant's trunk, elephants: drunk

Elsie Whitty: a titty
Eartha Kitts: tits

F

fairy bower: a shower
fancy sash: to bash

Farmer Giles: the piles

fiddles and flutes: the boots

fiddley-did: a quid, one pound sterling (obs.)

five by two: a Jew

five to two, five-ter: a Jew

fleas and itches: the pictures, cinema

fleas and scratches: matches

Flemington races: braces

flowery dell: a cell (prison)

forgive and forget: a cigarette

four by two: a Jew

Fred Astaire (1): a chair

Fred Astaire (2): the hair

Fred Astaire (3): a lair, a dandy

fried rice: the price

Frog and toad: the road, e.g. 'Hit the frog'

froth and bubble: a racing double, the daily double

G

gay and hearty: a party

George the Third: dog's turd

Germaine Greer: a beer

German band: the hand

Gerry Riddle: a piddle

Gertie Gitana: banana

giddy gout: a boy scout

giddy goat: the tote, the totalisator

ginger beer: a queer, a pervert

ginger beers: the ears

Goldsborough Mort: port (wine)

gone and forgotten: rotten

greasy mop, greasy: a cop, a policeman

green gages: wages

Gregory Peck: the neck, e.g. **'down
  the Gregory'**

Gregory Pecks: specs (glasses)

Gregory Peg: the leg

grey nurse: a purse

grim and gory: a story

grocer's cart: the heart

grumble and grunt: the cunt

Gungha Din: gin (drink)

Gypsie Lee: tea

H

half inch: to pinch, to steal

hammer and tack: a zac, sixpence
  (obs.)

hanky panky: cranky, silly

hansom cab: a scab, a non-unionist

happy hour: a shower

hard hit: a shit

Harold Holt (1):   salt

Harold Holt (2):   a bolt (abscond = he
  done a Harold Holt)

Hawkesbury Rivers: the cold shivers

heart and soul of the goanna: the
  varsovienna, a dance

Herby de Groote: a root, sexual intercourse

here and now: a Chow, a Chinaman

hers and hims: hymns

hickey hockey: a jockey

hi-diddle-diddle: a piddle

highland fling: string

hit and miss: a piss

Holy Ghost (1): the post, mail

Holy Ghost (2): toast

Holy Ghosts: fence posts

home on the range: change (money)

honky tonk: plonk, cheap wine

horse and cart (1): a fart

horse and cart (2): the start

horse and foal: the dole

horse's hoof: a poof, poofter, male homosexual

hot cross bun: the sun

hot potater: later

Huckleberry Finn: gin

I

I suppose: the nose
in between: a quean
I'm afloat: an overcoat

J

J. Arthur Rank: a wank
Jack and Jill (1): a dill, a fool
Jack and Jill (2): a hill
Jack Flash: hash (hasheesh)
Jack Rees: fleas
Jack Scratches: the matches
Jack Shay: to stay
Jack the Dancer: cancer
Jim Gerald: *The Herald*
Jimmy Britts: the shits
Jimmy Dancer: cancer
Jimmy Grant, Jimmy: an immigrant, a Pommy
Jimmy Lee: tea
Jimmy Riddle: a piddle
Joe Blake: a snake
Joe Blakes: the shakes, the D.T.s
Joe Hope: the soap
Joe Rocks: the socks
John Bull: a pull, to masturbate
John Hop, a John, the Johns: a cop, the cops, police
Johnny Cash: hash (hasheesh)

Johny Horner: a corner
Johnny Raper, a Johnny: newspaper
Juicy Fruit: a root (sexual intercourse)

K

Kembla Grange, Kembla: small change
Kelly Ned: the head
Kennedy rot: a sot
kerb and gutter: butter
Khyber Pass, Khyber: the arse
kid blister: sister
King Henry the Third: dog's turd
king hit: a shit
King of Spain: rain
kitchen sink: a drink
knock me silly, knock-me: a billy

L

lady from Bistol: a pistol
lamb's fry (1):   a neck tie
lamb's fry (fries) (2):   the eye(s)
Lane Cove: a stove

larrikin's hat: a fat, an erection of the penis

laughs and smiles: the piles

leg of pork: the stalk, the penis

lemon squash: a wash

let's rejoice: the voice

Lillian Gish: a dish

Lily of Lagoona: a schooner, of beer

lisp and stutter: butter

loop the loop, loopy the loop: soup

lump of lead (1)**:** bread

lump of lead (2)**:** the head

M

Mad Mick: a pick

Mallee root: a prostitute

Manchester Cities: titties

Marcus Clark: a shark

Mark Foy: a boy

Martin Place: the face

Micky Duck: a fuck

Micky Mouse: grouse, good-oh

Micky Spillane: a game

mild and meek: the cheek

mince pies: the eyes

Minnie Mouse: the house

misbehave: a shave

Mister Mutch: the crutch (groin)

Molly Maguire: a fire

Moreton Bay fig, a Moreton Bay: a gig, a fizzgig, an informer

Morts Dock: the cock, penis
mother and daughter: water
Mother Machree: tea
mother's joy: a boy
mud and ooze: booze
mud pies: the eyes
Mum and Dad: mad
Mum and Daddo: a shadow
Mutt and Jeff: deaf

N

nails and screws: news
Nancy Lee: a pee
napper tandy: a shandy
Nazi spy: a meat pie
near and far: a bar
Ned Kelly: the belly
Nelly Bligh (1): the trousers fly
Nelly Bligh(s) (2): the eye(s)
Nelly Kelly: the belly
Nelson Riddle, Nelson: a piddle
never better: a letter
Niagara Falls: the balls, testicles
Noah's Ark: a shark
north and south: the mouth
North Sydney: the kidney

O

ocean liner: cliner, a girl
oh my dear: beer
Old Black Joes: the toes
old china plate, old china: old mate
Old Jack Lang: rhyming slang
Oliver Twist: the wrist
one alone: a moan
one another: brother
ones and twos: shoes
Onkaparinga, Onka: a finger
optic nerve: a perv, a pervert
orchestra stalls (orchestras):   the balls
   (testes)
**Oscar Ash, Oscar Asche, Oscar Nash,
   Oscar, Okker:**   cash
Oxford scholar: a dollar

P

Pat Malone: alone, on one's own, e.g.
   **'all on my Pat Malone', 'I'm on my
   Pat'**
pay me rent: a tent
pear and quince: a prince
peas in the pot: hot
pen and ink: a stink
Penny Brown: a town
pickled pork: a walk
pig's arse: a glass

pig's ear: beer

pitch and toss: the boss

plates of meat: the feet

pinkity plonk: plonk, vin blanc, any wine

plum pud: good

post and rail: a fairy tale, a lie

pot and pan: the old man, husband

purple and mauve: the stove

Q

quiver and shake: a steak

R

rammy rousers: trousers

red hots: the trots, dysentery

Reg Grundy's (Reggy's): undies

rice and sago: a Dago, a Greek

Richard the Third, a Richard: a turd

Rickety Dick: the prick, a stick

Rickety Kate: a gate

River Murray: curry

River Murrays: worries

roaring horsetails: Aurora Australis

roaring rain: a train

roast pork: a talk

Roberta Flack: the sack, the bed. e.g. 'hit the Roberta'

rock and roll: the dole

rock and lurch: a church

role me in the gutter: butter
rolling deep: sleep
Rory O'Moore: the floor
roses red: a bed
Rosie Lee: tea
rubbity dub, rubbity: a pub
ruby moon: a spoon

S

Saint Louis Blues: shoes
Saint Vitus Dance: the pants
salty bananas: sultanas
Sandy Macnabs: the crabs, body lice
saucepan lids: kids
sausage roll: a goal, VFL football. e.g.
   'Kicked a sausage'
sausage and mash: cash. e.g. **'ain't**
   got a sausage'
Scotch tape: rape
sealing wax: tax
septic tank, septic: a Yank
shake and shiver: a river
short ease: the schottische (dance)
short squeeze: the schottische (dance)
shower of rain: a train
silly galoot: a root, sexual intercourse
silver spoon: the moon
sky rocket: the pocket
Slapsie Maxie: a taxi
slippery dip: lip, cheekiness
smash and grab: a cab

snake's hiss, snake's: a piss
soap and water: daughter
soft as silk: milk
South Sydney: a kidney
spire and steeple: people
squatter's daughter: water
steak and kidney: Sydney
steam tug (1): a pug, prize fighter
steam tug(s) (2): bug(s)
Steele Rudds: spuds, potatoes
Stevey Hart: a fart
stick of chalk: a walk
Stockton punt: the cunt
stop thief: beef
strangle and smother: mother
strum and stroll: the dole
submarine: a quean
Swannee Rivers (Swannees): the shivers
Sydney Harbour: a barber

T

tea leaf: a thief
tea leafing: thieving
teddy bear: a lair, a dandy
ten furlongs: daughter (a mile and a quarter)
ten to twos: shoes
these and those: toes
thick and thin: the skin
thief and robber: cobber

this and that: a bat, for cricket

three bags full: a lot of bull, a pack of lies

thunder and rain: a train

tiddly wink: a drink

Tiger Tim, Tiger: a swim

tin lid: a kid

tit for tat, titfer (1):   a hat

tit for tat (2):   a rat, non-unionist

to and from: a Pom, a Pommy

Tom and Sam: jam

Tom Thumb (1):   rum

Tom Thumb (2):   the drum, inside information

tom tit: a shit

tomato sauce: a horse

tomato sauces: the horses, horse races

ton o' my rocks: socks

tree and sap: a tap

trey bits: the shits

trouble and strife: the wife

twist and twirl: a girl

Two UEs (2UEs):   fleas

two wheeler: a sheila

Tyrone Power: a shower

U

Uncle Ned: bread

Uncle Willy, uncle: silly

up and under: chunder, to vomit

V

Var Susy Anne: varsovienna (dance)

Vera Lynn: the chin, gin

Victor Trumper: a bumper, a cigarette butt

violet crumble: tumble, take a tumble, to understand

virgin bride: a ride

W

Warwick Farm, Warwicks: the arm, arms, e.g. **'whiffy under the Warwicks'** = 'smelly under the arms'

Trouble and strife

wasp and bee: tea
Wellington boot: a root, sexual intercourse
Werris Creek, Werris: a Greek
whirling spray: a Wirraway, obsolete R.A.A.F. training plane
whistle and flute, whistle: a suit
willy wag: a swag
Winchcombe Carson: a parson
windjammer: a hammer
wiss wot: a piss pot
witchetty grub: a cub, boy scout
wombat: dead, hors de combat
woolly boof: a poof, a poofter

X

Xerox copy: Remembrance Day poppy

Y

Yogi Bear: boob lair, jail dandy
you and me: a pee
young and frisky: whisky

Z

Zane Grey: one's pay, pay packet, wages

Vocabulary

"Straight" to
Rhyming Slang

A

alone: on one's Pat Malone
Alsatian (dog): all stations
arm, the: Warwick Farm, Warwicks, e.g. 'wiffy under the Warwicks'
arse (1): bottle and glass
arse (2) Khyber Pass, Khyber
Aurora Australis: roaring horsetails

B

balls (testicles) (1): cobbler's awls, cobblers
balls (testicles) (2): Niagara Falls, Niagaras
balls (testicles) (3): orchestra stalls, orchestras
banana: Gertie Gitana
bar, a: near and far
barber (1): Coffs Harbour
barber (2): Sydney Harbour
bash, to: fancy sash
bat (cricket): this and that
bed (1): roses red
bed (2): = 'the sack': Roberta Flack, the Roberta
beef: stop thief
beer, a (1): a Germaine Greer
beer, a (2): oh my dear
belly (1): Darby Kelly
belly (2): Ned Kelly
belly (3): Nelly Kelly

belt, a: dark felt
bet, to have a: cast a net
billy, a: knock me silly
bolt, a (to abscond): Harold Holt
Bonox and rum: dad and mum
book: docker's hook
boots (1): daisy roots
boots (2): fiddles and flutes
boss, the: pitch and toss
bottle: Aristotle, Aris
bowler (cricket): Coca Cola
boy, a (1): Mark Foy
boy, a (2): mother's joy
braces: Flemington races
bread (1): lump o'lead
bread (2): Uncle Ned
brother: one another
bucket: dip and tuck it
bugs: steam tugs
bull, a load of: three bags full
bumper, a (cigarette end): Victor
   Trumper
butter (1): kerb and gutter
butter (2): lisp and stutter
butter (3): roll/chuck me in the gutter

C

cab, a: smash and grab
cancer: Jimmy Dancer or Jack the
   Dancer
carton: Bobby Matin

cash (1):   Oscar Ash, Oscar Nash, Oscar, Okker

cash (2):   sausage and mash. e.g. 'ain't got a sausage'

catalogue: cattle dog

Catholic: cattle tick

cell (prison):   flowery dell

chair: Fred Astaire

change (money):   Kembla Grange, Kembla

cheek (impertinence):   mild and meek

cheese (1):   Anne Louise

cheese (2):   cough and sneeze

cheque: duck's neck

chief, the (boss):   chunk o'beef, chunka

chin, the: Vera Lynn

chorus (of a song):   coalbox

Chow (Chinaman):   here and now

chunder (to vomit):   up and under

church: roll and lurch

cigger (cigarette):   African nigger

cigarette: forgive and forget

cliner (girlfriend):   ocean liner

cobber: thief and robber

cock (penis) (1):   eight day clock

cock (penis) (2):   Morts Dock

cold: brave and bold

cold shivers: Hawkesbury Rivers

concertina: constant screamer

cook, a: babbling brook, babbler

cop (policeman) (1):   greasy mop, greasy

cop (policeman) (2):   John Hop, a John

copper (policeman):   bottle and stopper

corner: Johnny Horner

crabs (body lice) (1):   Sandy McNabs
crabs (body lice) (2):   dribs and drabs
crabs (body lice) (3):   dibs and dabs
cranky: hanky panky
crap, a (shit):   Andy Capp

Andy Capp

crook (feeling unwell):   butcher's hook
crust: dirt grime and dust
crutch (the groin):   Mister Mutch
cub (boy scout):   witchetty grub
cunt (1):   grumble and grunt
cunt (2):   Stockton punt
cup: down and up
curry: River Murray

D

Dago: rice and sago
Darlinghurst: darling it hurts
daughter (1):   soap and water
daughter (2):   ten furlongs (= a mile and
   a quarter)
dead, *(hors de combat)*:   wombat
deaf (1):   A.I.F.
dead (2):   Mutt and Jeff

dice: cats and mice

dill (a fool) (1): Jack and Jill

dill (a fool) (2): Beecham's Pill

dinner: Derby winner

dip, a (pick pocket): cockies' clip

dish, a: Dorothy Gish, a Dorothy

dog: chock and log

dole, the (1): rock and roll

dole, the (2): strum and stroll

dole, the (3): horse and foal

dollar: Oxford scholar

double (racing): froth and bubble

drink, a (1): cuff link

drink, a (2): tiddly wink

drink, a (3): kitchen sink

drum, the (information) (1): deaf and dumb

drum, the (information) (2): Tom Thumb

drunk: elephant's trunk, elephants

dunny (lavatory): don't be funny

E

ears: ginger beers
eyes (1): mince pies
eyes (2): mud pies
eyes (3): lamb's fry (fries)
eyes (4): Nelly Bligh(s)

F

face: Martin Place
fairy tale (a lie): post and rail
fart (1): horse and cart
fart (2): Stevey Hart
fart (3): apple tart (he apple tarted)
fat, a (erection): larrikin's hat
feet: plates of meat
finger: onkaparinga
fire (1): Andy Maguire
fire (2): Barney Maguire
fire (3): Molly Maguire
firewood: do me good
fish, a: dirty dish
fit, to throw a: chuck a Charlie Britt, chuck a Charlie
fleas (1): Jack Rees
fleas (2): 2UEs

floor: Rory O'Moore

flower: Cobar shower

flush, a (poker): barmaid's blush

fly (of the trousers): Nelly Blye

french letter: don't forget her

fuck (1): Donald Duck

fuck (2): Mickey Duck

G

game, a: Micky Spillane

gate: Rickety Kate

gay, a (homosexual): Doris Day

gig, a (fizzgig, an informer): Morton Bay fig, Morton Bay

gin (1): Huckleberry Finn, Vera Lynn

gin (drink) (2): Gungha Din

girl: twist and twirl

glass, a (drinking):   pig's arse

goal, a (V.F.L. football):   a sausage roll. e.g. 'kicked a sausage'

good: plum pud

goon, a (silly person):   egg and spoon

Greek, a: Werris Creek, a Werris

grouse (good):   Micky Mouse

guard (train):   Christmas card

guts, the: comic cuts, the comics

H

hair (1):   Dublin Fair

hair (2):   Fred Astaire

hammer: windjammer

hand, the: German band

hash, hasheesh (1):   Jack Flash

hash, hasheesh (2):   Johnny Cash

hat (1):   barrel of fat

hat (2):   tit for tat, titfer

head, the (1):   Kelly Ned

head (2):   lump of lead

heart: grocer's cart

Herald, The: Jim Gerald

hill, a: Jack and Jill

horse (1):   tomato sauce

horse (2):   apple sauce

horses, the (horse races):   tomato sauces

hot: peas in the pot

house: Minnie Mouse

hymns: hers and hims

I

immigrant, an (a Pommy):   a Jimmy
   Grant, a Jimmy, a Pommy
in the know: in the Brown Joe

J

jam: Tom and Sam
Jew (1):   five by two
Jew (2):   five to two
Jew (3):   four by two
jockey: hickey hockey

K

Aunty Meg

keg: Aunty Meg
kid(s):   tin lid(s), saucepan lids

kidney: South Sydney
king, the: ding a ling
Kings Cross: pitch and toss

L

lair (dandy): Fred Astaire
lair (boob lair): Yogi Bear
lair (mug lair): Teddy Bear
later: hot potater
leak, a (to urinate): bubble and squeak
leeches: cries and screeches
leg, the (1): Gregory Peg
leg (2): clothes pegs
legs (3): Dutch pegs
letter (1): don't forget her
letter (2): never better
lip (cheekiness): slippery dip
loan, a: Derby and Joan
look, a (1): butcher's hook
look, a (2): Captain Cook
louse: Mickey Mouse

M

mad: mum and dad
marry, to: cash and carry
matches (1): fleas and scratches
matches (2): Jack Scratches
mate: china plate, china
meat pie: Nazi spy

milk: soft as silk

miss, a (cricket, a missed catch):   a cheesy kiss

missus, the: cheese and kisses, old cheese

moan, a: one alone

money (1):   Bugs Bunny

money (2):   bees and honey

moon, the: silver spoon

mother: strangle and smother, strangle

mouth, the: north and south

N

neck, the (1):   bushell and peck

neck, the (2):   Gregory Peck

neck tie: lamb's fry

news: nails and screws

newspaper: Johnny Raper, a Johnny

nose: I suppose

number: cucumber

O

old man (husband or father):   pot and pan

overcoat: I'm afloat

P

pants: Saint Vitus' dance

parson: Winchcombe Carson

party: gay and hearty

pee (1):   Dicky Lee

pee (2):   Nancy Lee

pee (3):   sweet Marie

pee (4):   you and me

people: spire and steeple

perv (pervert):   optic nerve

phone: see under 'telephone'

pick, a: a mad Mick

pictures (cinema):   fleas and itches

piddle (1):   Hi diddle diddle

piddle (2):   Jimmy Riddle

piddle (3):   Nelson Riddle, a Nelson

pie, meat: Nazi spy

piles (haemorrhoids) (1):   Farmer Giles

piles (haemorrhoids) (2):   laughs and
  smiles

pinch, to: to half inch

pipe (smoking):   cherry ripe

piss (1):   angel's kiss

piss (2):   hit and miss

piss (3):   snake's hiss, a snake's

pissed (drunk) (1):   Adrian Quist

pissed (2):   Brahms and Liszt

piss-pot: wiss wot

pistol: lady from Bristol

plonk (cheap wine):   honky tonk, plinkity
  plonk

pocket: sky rocket

police, the: ducks and geese

Pom, Pommy: to and from

Pommy: a Jimmy (from Jimmy Grant =
  immigrant)

Horse's hoof

poof (poofter) (1): cow's hoof
poof (poofter) (2): horse's hoof
poof (poofter) (3): woolly boof
Poppy, Remembrance: a Xerox copy
port (wine): Goldsborough Mort
post (mail): holy ghost
posts (fence): holy ghosts
pox, the: boots and sox
price, the (1): curry and rice
price, the (2): fried rice
prick, the: rickety Dick
prince, a: pear and quince
prostitute: Mallee root
pub: rubbity dub, rubbity
pug, a (prize fighter): steam tug
pull, a (masturbate) (1): cotton wool

pull, a (masturbate) (2):   John Bull
purse: a grey nurse

Q

quid (one pound, old
   currency):   fiddley-did
queer (gay):   ginger beer
quean (1):   an in between
quean (2):   a submarine

R

race, not in the: not in the Charlie
   Chase
railway line: ball of twine
rain: King of Spain
rape: Scotch tape
rat (1) (informer):   cabbage tree hat
rat (2) (non-unionist):   tit for tat
razor: a Dawn Frazer
ride, a: a virgin bride
river (1):   a bullock's liver
river (2):   shake and shiver
road: frog and toad

root, a (sexual intercourse) (1):   Herby de Groote

root, a (2):   silly galoot

root, a (3):   Wellington boot

root, a (4):   Juicy Fruit

rotten: gone and forgotten

rum (1):   dad and mum

rum (2):   Tom Thumb

run away (abscond):   Botany Bay, e.g. 'do a Botany'

S

salt: Harold Holt

sauce: dead horse

scab (non-unionist):   hansom cab

scarf: cry and laugh

schooner (of beer):   Lily of Lagoona

schottische (dance) (1):   short ease

scottische (2):   short squeeze

scout: giddy gout

shadow: mum and daddo

shakes, the (D.T.s) (1):   ducks and drakes

shakes, the (D.T.s) (2):   Joe Blakes, the

shandy: Napper Tandy

shark (1):   Marcus Clarke

shark (2):   Noah's ark

shave (1):   Dad and Dave

shave (2):   dig a grave

shave (3):   a misbehave

Sheila (1):   Charlie Wheeler, a Charlie

Sheila (2):   a two wheeler

shirt: dinky dirt
shit (1): Edgar Britt
shit (2): a hard hit
shit (3): a king hit
shit (4): a Dinny Hayes-er = a king hit
shit (5): a tom tit

shits, the (1):   the Jimmy Britts
shits, the (2):   the trey bits
shivers, the: Swannee Rivers, Swannees
shoes (1):   ones and twos
shoes (2):   ten to twos
shoes (3):   Saint Louis Blues
shower, a (1):   Fairy Bower
shower, a (2):   happy hour
shower, a (3):   Tyrone Power
shower, a (4):   Eiffel Tower
silly: Uncle Willy
sister (1):   blood blister
sister (2):   kid blister
six, a (cricket): a Dorothy Dix
skin: thick and thin
slang: old Jack Lang
sleep (1):   Bo Peep
sleep (2):   rolling deep
small change: Kembla Grange
snake: Joe Blake
soap (1):   Bob Hope
soap (2):   Cape of Good Hope
soap (3):   Joe Hope
socks (1):   almond rocks
socks (2):   Bobby Rocks
socks (3):   Curly locks
socks (4):   Joe Rocks
socks (5):   ton o' my rocks
soup: loop the loop, loopy the loop
sot, a: a Kennedy rot
specs (glasses):   Gregory Pecks
spoon: ruby moon
spuds (1):   Captain Bloods

spuds (2):   Steele Rudds
stairs: apples and pears
stalk (the penis):   leg of pork
start, the: the horse and cart
stay, to: Jack Shay
steak: quiver and shake
stick, a: clickety-click
stink: pen and ink
stove (1):   purple and mauve
stove (2):   Lane Cove
story, a: grim and gory
story, a crim's: John Dory
string: Highland fling
suit, a (1):   a bag of fruit
suit, a (2):   whistle and flute, a whistle
sulky (vehicle):   big and bulky
sultanas: salty bananas
sun, the: hot cross bun/currant bun
swag: willy wag
swim (1):   dark and dim
swim (2):   Tiger Tim, a tiger
Sydney (1):   steak and kidney
Sydney (2):   bullock's kidney

T

table (1):   Betty Grable
table (2):   Cain and Abel
talk, a: roast pork
tap, a: a tree and sap
tats (the teeth):   cricket bats
tax: sealing wax

taxi: a slapsie Maxie
tea (1): Dicky Lee
tea (2): Gypsie Lee
tea (3): Jimmy Lee
tea (4): Mother Machree
tea (5): Rosie Lee
tea (6): wasp and bee
telephone (1): Al Capone
telephone (2): dog and bone
telephone (3): Eau de Cologne
tent: pay me rent
terrified: bona fide

Gypsie Lee

thief: a tea leaf

thieving: tea leafing

thinkbox (the head): bundle of sox

time, the: birdslime

tip, a (racing): egg flip

tits: Eartha Kitts

titties (1): Bristol Cities, Bristols

titties (2): Manchester Cities

titty, a: Elsie Whitty

toes (1): buttons and bows

toes (2): Old Black Joes

toes (3): these and those

tool (the penis): April fool

tote (totalisator): giddy goat

towel (1): Baden Powell

towel (2): Bob Powell

town: Penny Brown

tram: bread and jam

train (1): roaring rain

train (2): thunder and rain

train (3): a shower of rain

trey (threepence, old currency): Alma
  Grey

trots, the (diarrhoea): the red hots

trousers (1): dead wowsers

trousers (2): rammy rousers

tub, a (a bath): Bib and Bub

tumble, take a (to understand): violet
  crumble

turd (dog's) (1): a George the Third

turd (dog's) (2): a King Henry the Third

turd, a (3): a Richard the Third, a
  Richard

U

undies: Reg Grundy's

V

varsovienna (the dance) (1):   heart and
soul of the goanna

varsovienna (the dance) (2):   arse over
header

varsovienna (the dance) (3):   Var Susy
Anna

vin blanc (plonk):   plinkity plonk

voice: let's rejoice

W

wages: green gages

walk (1):   pickled pork

walk (2):   stick of chalk

wall: bat and ball

wank, a: a J. Arthur Rank

wash, a: a lemon squash

water (1):   mother and daughter

water (2):   squatter's daughter

whisky: young and frisky

wife: trouble and strife

Wirraway (aeroplane):   whirling spray

Wog (Italian) (1):   Alsatian dog

Wog (Italian) (2):   chocolate frog

Mother and daughter

work: dodge and shirk
worry, worries: River Murray(s)
wrist, the: Oliver Twist

Y

Yank, a (an American):   a septic tank, a septic

Z

zac (sixpence, old currency):   a hammer and tack